W9-DBF-627

ZOOM In on Animals!

Boa Constrictors
Up Close

Carmen Bredeson

Enslow Elementary

CONTENTS

WORDS TO KNOW

constrictors (cuhn STRIK terz)—Snakes that squeeze animals to kill them for food.

digest (dye JEST)—To use food in the body.

poison (POY zuhn)—Something that causes sickness or death.

prey (PRAY)—An animal that is killed for food.

squeeze (SKWEEZ)—To press and hold very tightly.

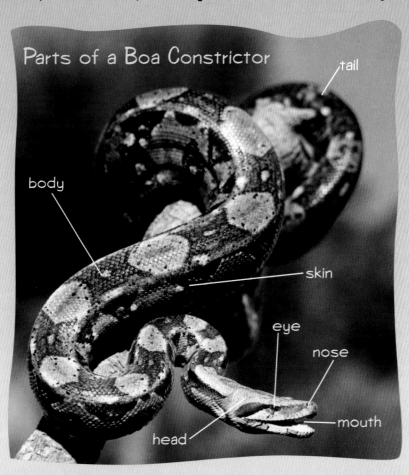

Parts of a Boa Constrictor

tail

body

skin

eye

nose

mouth

head

BIG BOA

Boa constrictors are very big snakes. Some grow to be fifteen feet long.

Boa constrictor skin is brown like the forest floor. Other boas are green like leaves. Hiding in the forest is easy for boas.

North
America

Central
America

South
America

Most boas live in the
forests of Central and
South America.

BOA EYES

Snakes never blink or close their eyes. They do not have eyelids. Clear skin covers the boa's eyes to keep out dirt and bugs. Snake eyes are always watching.

BOA TONGUE

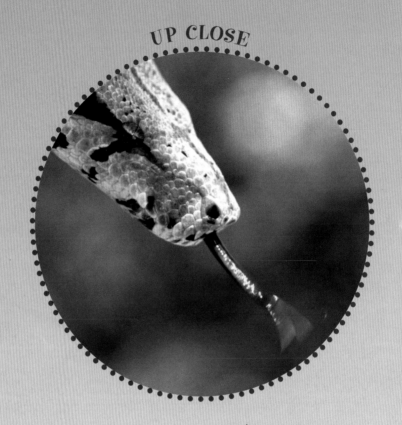

UP CLOSE

A snake uses its tongue for smelling.
It flicks its tongue in and out, in and out.
This brings air into its mouth. The snake's
brain knows if the air smells like danger
or dinner.

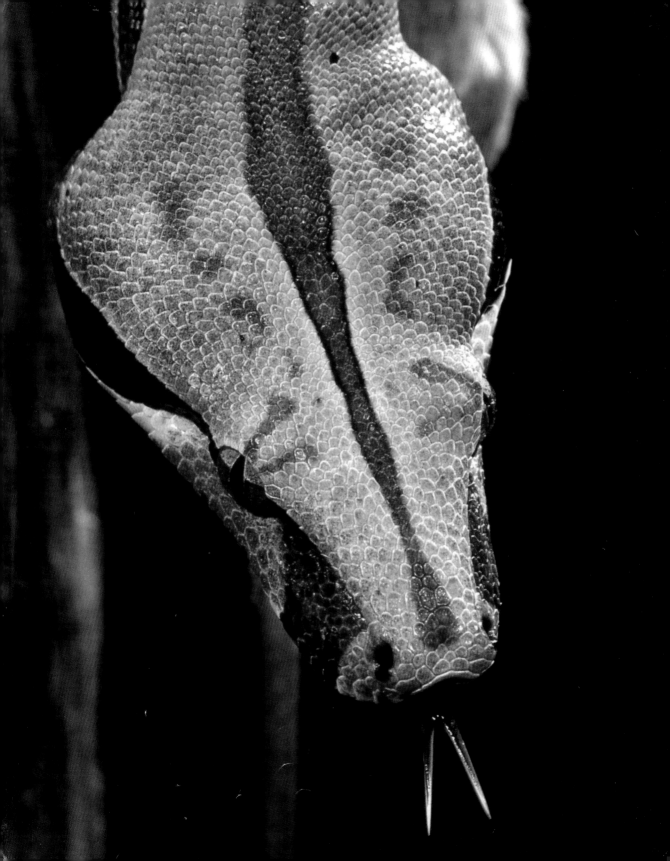

BOA TAIL

Young emerald tree boa. (It turns green when it grows up.)

Boas do not crawl very fast. They hang from trees or hide in bushes, waiting for a meal. A boa tail loops around and around a branch. When an animal passes by, the tail quickly lets go of the branch.

Amazon tree boa ▶

BOA TEETH

Boa skeleton

Boas eat animals such as rats, lizards, birds, monkeys, and frogs. Boas bite their prey quickly with sharp teeth. The teeth point backward, so the animal cannot get loose.

Emerald tree boa ▶

BOA ATTACK

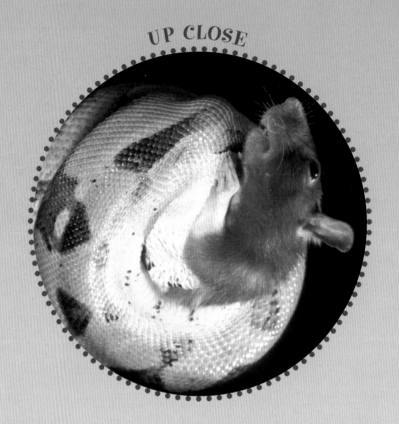

Boas do not shoot poison into their prey.
They curl around and around the struggling
animal. Then they squeeze, squeeze,
squeeze. Soon the animal dies because it
cannot breathe.

This Amazon tree boa
is squeezing a bird. ▶

BOA MOUTH

The boa's jaw drops down. Then its mouth
can OPEN WIDE and swallow the animal whole.
It takes a long time for a boa to swallow its meal.
The animal makes a lump in the snake's body
until the snake digests it.

BOA BABIES

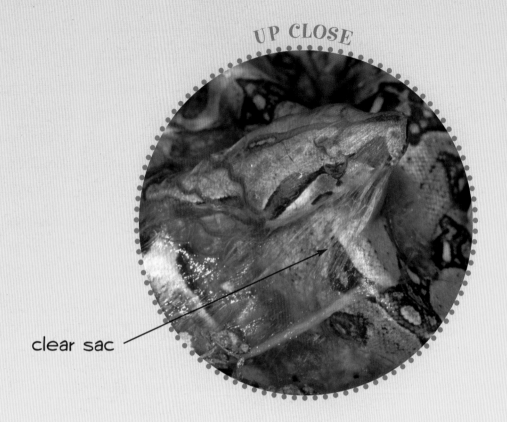

clear sac

Twenty to fifty baby snakes grow in their mother's body. They grow in clear sacs that look like bubbles.

Most snakes are hatched from eggs, but not boas! They are born alive and ready to hunt.

BOA SKIN

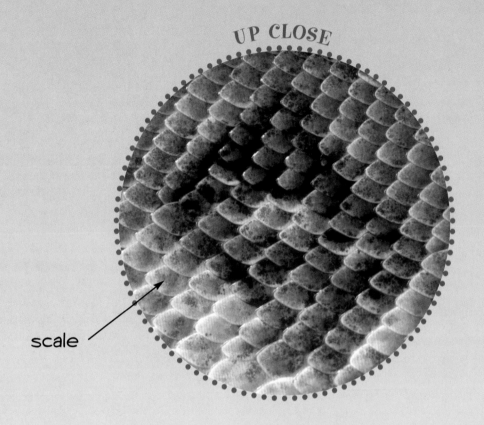

scale

Boa skin is made of scales. As a boa grows, its skin gets too small for its body. New skin grows under the old skin. The boa crawls out of its old skin and wiggles away into the forest.

old skin

BOA LIFE CYCLE

LIVE BABY
20 to 50 babies
are born at a time.

YOUNG SNAKE
It takes 3 years
to grow up.

ADULT SNAKE
It lives to be about
20 years old.

LEARN MORE

Books

Doeden, Matt. *Boa Constrictors*. Minneapolis, Minn.: Capstone Press, 2005.

Longenecker, Theresa. *Who Grows Up in the Rain Forest?* Minneapolis, Minn.: Picture Window Books, 2003.

Schlaepfer, Gloria. *Pythons and Boas*. Danbury, Conn.: Franklin Watts, 2003.

Web Sites

Oakland Zoo. *Animals A–Z: Boa Constrictor.* <http://www.oaklandzoo.org/atoz/azboa.html>

San Diego Zoo. *Boa: Quick Facts.* <http://www.sandiegozoo.org/animalbytes/ t-boa.html>

INDEX

Series Literacy Consultant:
Allan A. De Fina, Ph.D.
Past President of the New Jersey Reading Association
Professor, Department of Literacy Education
New Jersey City University

Science Consultant:
John Kinkaid
Animal Care Manager
San Diego Zoo
San Diego, California

Science note: Boa constrictor is the common name for any snake of the genus *Boa*. Although the individual species *Boa constrictor* is highlighted in this book, photos of some other *Boa* species are included.

Note to Parents and Teachers: The Zoom In on Animals! series supports the National Science Education Standards for K–4 science. The Words to Know section introduces subject-specific vocabulary words, including pronunciation and definitions. Early readers may need help with these new words.

For Andrew and Charlie, our wonderful grandsons

Enslow Elementary, an imprint of Enslow Publishers, Inc.

Enslow Elementary® is a registered trademark of Enslow Publishers, Inc.

Copyright © 2006 by Carmen Bredeson

All rights reserved.

No part of this book may be reproduced by any means without the written permission of the publisher.

Library of Congress Cataloging-in-Publication Data

Bredeson, Carmen.
    Boa constrictors up close / Carmen Bredeson.
        p. cm. — (Zoom in on animals!)
    Includes bibliographical references and index.
    ISBN 0-7660-2498-9 (hardcover)
    1. Boa constrictor—Juvenile literature. I. Title. II. Series.
    QL666.O63B74 2006
    597.96'78—dc22
                            2005003329

Printed in the United States of America

10 9 8 7 6 5 4 3 2 1

To Our Readers: We have done our best to make sure all Internet Addresses in this book were active and appropriate when we went to press. However, the author and the publisher have no control over and assume no liability for the material available on those Internet sites or on other Web sites they may link to. Any comments or suggestions can be sent by e-mail to comments@enslow.com or to the address on the back cover.

Cover photos: Zoological Society of San Diego (large image); © Chris Mattison; Frank Lane Picture Agency /CORBIS (eye); © Joe McDonald/Tom Stack & Assoc. Inc. (tongue); © Joe McDonald / Animals Animals (skin).

Photo credits: © A. Brando/OSF/ Animals Animals, p. 21; © Betty and Nathan Cohen / Visuals Unlimited, p. 12; © Michael & Patricia Fogden /CORBIS, p. 4–5; © Francois Gohier / ardea.com, p. 3; © Brian Kenney, p. 18; © Chris Mattison; Frank Lane Picture Agency /CORBIS, p. 6; © Joe McDonald / Animals Animals, pp. 14, 15, 20; © Joe McDonald/CORBIS, p. 17; Joe McDonald/Tom Stack & Associates, Inc., p. 9; © Joe and Mary Ann McDonald / Visuals Unlimited, p. 11; © Jim Merli / Visuals Unlimited, p. 16; Joel Sartore/National Geographic Image Collection, p. 8; Jany Sauvanet / Photo Researchers, Inc., p. 10; © Geoff Trinder / ardea.com, p. 19; © Peter Weimann / Animals Animals, p. 13; © Jim Zuckerman /CORBIS, p. 7.

Enslow Elementary
an imprint of
Enslow Publishers, Inc.
40 Industrial Road   PO Box 38
Box 398   Aldershot
Berkeley Heights, NJ 07922   Hants GU12 6BP
USA   UK
http://www.enslow.com